WIL

SOUTHERN
OKLAHOMA
Library System
Ardmore, Oklahoma

10/17

D1712459

"How does he know what they looked like?"

WITHDRAWN FROM
SOUTHERN OKLAHOMA
LIBRARY SYSTEM

big & SMALL

Original Korean text by Myeong-hwa Yu
Illustrations by Yeon-joo Kim
Korean edition © Aram Publishing

This English edition published by big & SMALL in 2017
by arrangement with Aram Publishing
English text edited by Scott Forbes
English edition © big & SMALL 2017

Distributed in the United States and Canada by
Lerner Publishing Group, Inc.
241 First Avenue North
Minneapolis, MN 55401 U.S.A.
www.lernerbooks.com

All rights reserved

ISBN: 978-1-925235-25-8

Printed in Korea

Putting Faces to Names

THE ART OF RAPHAEL

Written by Myeong-hwa Yu

Illustrated by Yeon-joo Kim

Edited by Scott Forbes

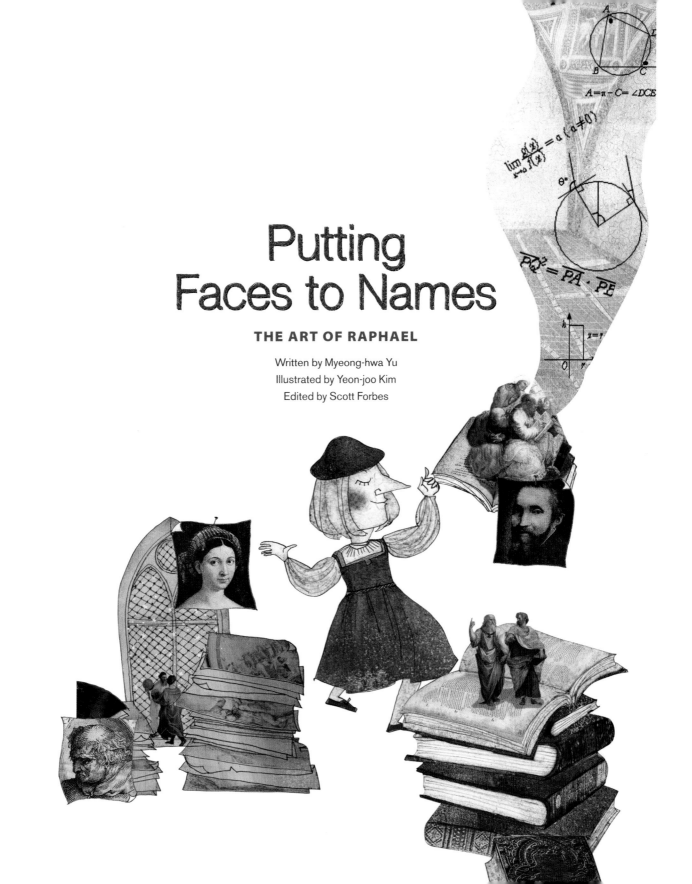

My name is Raphael and I'm one of
Italy's most important artists. Yes, I am!
One day, the Pope asked me to come
to his church, St. Peter's Basilica
in Rome. He wanted me to paint a
picture of the world's greatest scholars
for his library in his palace.
It was a great honor, and I said
I would be proud to do it.

6

7

8

I went to visit the Pope's library
with my assistant, John.
It was even bigger than I had expected,
with long walls and a domed ceiling.
"It's going to have to be a very big
painting," I told John.
Even for me, it was a challenge.
But then I quickly worked out what
I was going to do.
"It's a piece of cake," I said to John.

On our way out we saw another painter, Michelangelo. I'd heard that he had also been summoned by the Pope and asked to paint the ceiling of a chapel in the palace. Like me, he's quite brilliant and supremely confident. There's no way he would have said no.

Now we both have our tasks.
Let's see who's the better artist!

To fill up all that space in the Pope's library, I reckoned I needed to paint at least 50 scholars. It was time to do some research!

I went to Rome's biggest library and looked through hundreds of books. There were so many great scholars. How could I decide which ones to paint?

But I'm quite a scholar myself, and it didn't take me long to work it out! First, I thought, I'll start with the mathematicians. Mathematics is the basis of all science and invention, so it was important to have mathematicians. I was sure the Pope would like that!

I'm quite a deep thinker too, and I knew I had to include a few philosophers — the scholars who taught us how to think.

17

And I knew I couldn't leave out the astronomers, who
studied the skies, the stars, the Sun, the whole universe.
"What do you think?" I said to John.
"Sounds good to me!" he replied.

I'm a fair man and quite modern in my attitudes,
so I wanted to include some female scholars. I found
a few who had outshone their male rivals.

Finally, I counted all the scholars.
"Fifty-four. That will do. Time to get started!"

First I painted the school in Athens where the scholars were going to gather. Then I started working on the figures. I painted their bodies and robes. But when I got to their faces, I couldn't go any farther. What on earth did they look like? There were no pictures of them in any books.

20

21

"Hmm," I thought. "Michelangelo must be in the same position. He's been asked to paint people from the Bible and nobody knows what they looked like either."

John and I sneaked round to the chapel to see how Michelangelo was doing. And there he was, at the top of his ladder, painting in the faces, like he knew these people well and saw them every day.

"That's it!" I said to John. "Paint people you know."

If I may say so myself, it was
quite a brilliant thought I'd had.
I started looking for models
for the scholars in my painting.

Who's face should I give to
the great philosopher Plato?
Perhaps the Pope's face?
No, I'd use the face of that master
of painting, Leonardo da Vinci.

Somewhere I needed to include the face of
the architect Bramante, because I'd heard
he had recommended me to the Pope.
He's a smart guy, so I decided to make
him the mathematician Euclid.

Then I decide to sneak my girlfriend in
as one of the female scholars!

I wondered whether to include Michelangelo?
He's a terrible show-off, but he is
a skilled artist and he does
have a few good ideas.
So I put him in too.

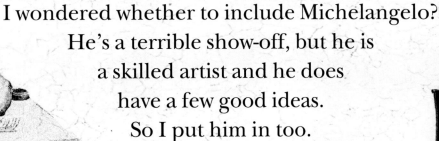

26

After many hours of work, I finished the painting. Then the Pope organized a grand reception for all the most important people in Rome to view his new artwork. He was delighted with it and said it made his library the greatest in the world.

He liked to show off his knowledge. He pointed out each and every scholar and explained who they all were.

Every so often he smiled at me. I nodded and smiled back at him.

The School of Athens (1509–11),
Apostolic Palace,
Vatican City, Rome, Italy

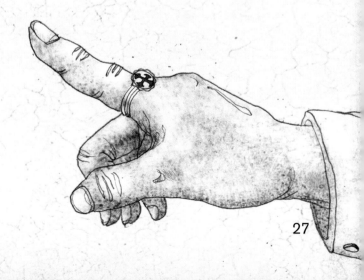

Suddenly, the Pope stopped talking
and stared hard at the painting.
He had recognized two faces: those
of Michelangelo and … me!

He turned toward me with a stern face.
I shrugged my shoulders and said,
"Your Holiness, only a truly great artist
can gather all these scholars in one
painting. And that's why I should be
included too!"

A smile broke across the Pope's face,
then he roared with laughter. "Raphael,
you are impudent … but brilliant!"

I had to agree.

28

Grace and imagination

Self-Portrait (1506), Uffizi
Gallery, Florence, Italy
This painting shows the artist
around the age of 23.

Raphael painted works of astonishing grace and beauty. For this he became known as "the prince of painters." He was born Raffaello Sanzio in 1483, in Urbino in central Italy. His mother died when he was eight and after that he was brought up by his father, Giovanni Santi, who was very strict. Santi was a successful artist whose paintings were popular with wealthy nobles. He had begun teaching his son to paint when Raphael was very young.

Learning from the masters

Sadly, Giovanni passed away when Raphael was just 11 years old. Raphael then left his home town and became an apprentice to another famous painter, Perugino, in the town of Perugia. Raphael was already a skilled artist, but he learned even more from Perugino. They worked on many paintings together, in towns all over central Italy. By the time he was 21, Raphael had painted a work that is still recognized as one of his masterpieces, *The Marriage of the Virgin*, completed in 1504.

Madonna d'Orléans
(1506), Musée Condé,
Chantilly, France
Raphael made many
beautiful paintings of Mary
with the infant Jesus.

Portrait of Maddalena Doni (1506), Palazzo Pitti, Florence, Italy
This portrait shows the influence of Leonardo da Vinci on Raphael. The woman's soft smile and slightly crooked posture, and the landscape in the background, are very like those in Leonardo's famous painting *The Mona Lisa*.

Soon Raphael felt he had learned as much as he could from Perugino. He moved to Florence, a major center of art in Italy at that time. There he studied the works of many artists, but particularly those of Leonardo da Vinci and Michelangelo. He learned a lot from their paintings and copied some of their techniques. But whereas Leonardo's and Michelangelo's paintings tended to be dark and gloomy, Raphael's paintings were usually bright, beautiful, graceful, and happy.

Working in Rome
In 1508, the Pope, Julius II, invited Raphael to work in Rome, and it was there that Raphael painted many of his masterpieces. He was asked to paint works for palaces and churches, to create backdrops for theatrical performances, and even design large buildings, including churches and palaces. These activities made him well known and his works became much loved by the Roman public.

Raphael's most famous works in Rome are the many frescoes he painted for the Pope's private apartments in the Vatican palace. These include *The School of Athens*, which was part of a series about scholars. Today the four rooms he decorated are known as the Raphael Rooms.

Early death
Tragically, Raphael died suddenly in 1520, on what may have been his 37th birthday. Huge crowds attended his funeral at the Vatican and he was buried in the Pantheon, a famous ancient temple in the center of Rome. It was a truly great honor for a much-loved artist.

1483
Born in Urbino, Italy

1502–03
Studies under Perugino

1504
Moves to Florence

1508
Pope Julius II invites Raphael to Rome and asks him to decorate his apartments

1513
Pope Julius II dies but Raphael continues to work for his successor, Leo X

1515
After Bramante's death, Raphael becomes Rome's most important architect

1520
Dies suddenly, aged 37

A closer look

The people in the painting

In his painting *The School of Athens*, Raphael showed 54 scholars from ancient times gathered in a great hall in Athens, Greece. Let's take a closer look at the painting and find out who Raphael used as his models for some of these famous figures.

1 Diogenes A philosopher who lived a simple life. He said being good was better than being rich. When Alexander the Great (see 5, below) asked Diogenes if there was anything he could do for him, he replied, "Yes, stop blocking the sunlight."

2 Heraclitus A philosopher who talked about how nature is endlessly changing. Raphael used Michelangelo as his model for this figure and showed him wearing Roman-style clothes.

3 Pythagoras A famous mathematician, he believed numbers were at the root of everything in this world. He created the famous mathematical formula called the "Pythagorean Theorem," which is still taught in schools today.

4 Hypatia A great female scholar, Hypatia taught mathematics, astronomy, and philosophy in Alexandria, Egypt.

5 Alexander the Great The king of Macedonia, near Greece, he conquered Persia and India to form a great empire. Aristotle (see 8) was his tutor.

6 Socrates A great philosopher of ancient Greece who was famous for his saying "Know thyself." Socrates believed that if people recognized their faults and tried to live in a truthful way, the world would become a more peaceful place.

7 Plato Another very famous philosopher, Plato was a student of Socrates (see 6). He founded the philosophy school known as the Academy, in Athens. Raphael used the artist and inventor Leonardo da Vinci as his model for Plato.

8 Aristotle Another great philosopher, Aristotle wrote on almost every subject and made many contributions to the early study of science and nature.

9 Raphael The man in the black hat standing talking to other scholars is a portrait of Raphael himself.

10 Sodoma Also known as Giovanni Bazzi, Sodoma worked with Raphael in Rome and was much influenced by him.

11 Zoroaster A philosopher and prophet who lived in ancient Persia, he founded a religion, Zoroastrianism, that is still around today.

12 Ptolemy A famous Greek astronomer, mathematician, geographer, and philosopher. He famously taught that the Sun and stars orbited the Earth.

13 Euclid A great mathematician whose works are still consulted today. As a model for Euclid, Raphael used the architect Donato Bramante, who had recommended Raphael to the Pope.

The School of Athens (1509–11),
Apostolic Palace,
Vatican City, Rome, Italy

"I think Raphael deserved to be in that painting."